"I can't express how blessed I feel to both help others and do what I love simultaneously. My gratitude goes out to my parents, sister, grandmother, friends at home, and friends at medical school for their help, guidance, and support. You all mean the world to me. I am also grateful to the patients and practitioners that I have met and who have inspired me so deeply."

Benjamin Andrew Casola 9/30/2015

Contents

Not Forgotten

A broken man I used to be
long before I could see
that with the bad, hope arrives
and with it faith always thrives.
In times of doubt or fearful dread,
those words inside me must be said
to quell that beast of spiteful aim
and give me poise to win this game.
Cusps of wind soon fight my tears
as mind-glued scenes flee through years.
Without courage, we would not fly
past wilted tops of treeless sky.
For even though my love is lost,
I cannot risk the painful cost
of leaving that which I adore,
the thought of love evermore.

The Eyes of a Survivor

"There's a Lithuanian saying: 'I sell for what I bought'. You know the hardest part? It was never telling anyone who you were."

As she said this, I adjusted my stethoscope so as to lighten it—maybe even conceal it.

"Escaping the Holocaust bears no great emblem on me. The only thing I inherited was a duty to honor my grandmother. She not only let me go, but even gave me the push that no one else would dare provide.

In 1941, the day that changed my life started at 5 A.M. A beaten, soot-covered teenager fell upon our doorstep, barely able to gasp for air, let alone warn us. Now that gunfire had crept to the ghetto, I peeled away my star. My grandmother, who was 82, examined me as I prepared to go. Her solemn eminence became a harbinger for what was to come.

'Are you leaving?' my grandmother asked me.

I grasped her hands, saying nothing.

'Good for you," she exclaimed.

I felt ashamed because I knew that she would not leave this poor boy. She wouldn't let him die alone. Soon after I left, they passed away together."

She looked down to release the thought, turned up at me, and attempted to smile.

"You are a first year, right?"

I pushed aside my medical equipment and pulled my chair closer, turning my scribbled pages to a blank section. I nodded, signaling her to resume her story.

"My first husband was taken from me during those rougher times. Out of concern for my well-being, one of his distant cousins gave me her identity to disguise who I once was. Two years later, I met my second husband, Frederick. Being in the German army, he sent me off to his father, a veteran, for safety. In return, I revealed who I really was.

The cards were his now, and my doubts persisted. What if this was a trap? Things could have changed. Nonetheless, my trust was firm, my exodus faithful. Watching the tail-lights drift away, my safe haven presented itself. I knocked on the door. A wide, stocky man with circular spectacles waddled out. He adjusted his glasses and stared into my eyes.

'Welcome home, child," he told me.

My head fell onto his chest. He knew who I was and didn't care. He just wanted to protect me."

I didn't know what to say. There were so many questions buzzing around in my head.

"What about your family?" I finally asked.

"I have no family, just my loves and memories. There is nothing needed to be kept here on this earth after my passing. My only hope is that time keeps my mind fresh enough to never let the past leave me before I leave it."

Jasmine

To walk through fire and remain unscathed
falls short of the one who learns from pain,
finding the waters of wisdom unbathed
to mend her scars and ascend the mundane.
Lifted beyond, my rara avis soars—
brightening the shrouds in radiant flare.
Mending a cold world with her fiery stores,
undaunted light with the earth she will share.
Many will see and admire her sheen,
but I know inside lies a heart pristine.

Responsibility

Sails adjusted to the wind,
directionless pages will rescind
against the walls of my mind
each time I look far behind.
Wandering with pen in hand,
from then to here I understand
what went wrong but not how
I could have made it better now.
Dwelling in thoughts, I do contend
with things I know were just pretend.
There is a chance to start anew,
knowing redemption might ensue.
Yes, it's scary and hard to try
forgiving myself for every lie
I made to myself and those I know.
To me, great amnesty they bestow.

Thich Nhat Hanh

Each morning,
we build our bones
hoping that
the ceaseless pounding
beyond those hills
stays at sea
as an idea
never gaining enough
power to make us
writhe with regret.

Under Bedrock

My nation falls upon a moor,
not knowing if it can endure—
not knowing if it can create
with so much to anticipate.
Buried and trapped beneath this land
I know I'll never understand,
flickers tell of something great—
the chance to finally sit and wait.
Into my picture, past the blue,
arises out this brighter hue.
Out of darkness, hope becomes
a prophet to which doubt succumbs.

Rewriting Medicine

Each torn bit of legislation
drags its spine along the ground,
looking up naïvely like a child
playing with power tools.
Innocence, adulterated
in one rapid splash of blame,
makes us all believe
our policies are unique.
Eerie similarities
we share so well
let us beam with hypocrisy
when we try to separate
without seeing how much
our goals quietly align.
Surprising, yes.
Almost an anthem,
our diagnoses ring out.
Somehow the word law
overtakes empathy.
Leer over my shoulder
in the midst of surgery,
and maybe we can
come to an agreement.

Grandma's Perspective

Antonia didn't know it, but farms would impregnate her brain with lasting beauty. This time would not fade as memory often does. What appeared as an evanescent feeling would grow inside her mind, body, and soul. As clichéd as it sounds, today she speaks of Italy as if it is down the road. As if Zia Adelina is our neighbor—her actions constantly a conversation topic. This is how it has been as far back as I can recall.

Her exercises in optimism are far from planned. On the contrary, they come naturally to her. Trying to rationalize this would make a madman out of anyone. Maybe it was Brooklyn. Perhaps Calabria. Either way, you are hard pressed to bring her down.

Chopin

I strike the keys and they play
the attitudes I've kept away
in unknown pieces of myself.
Where no treads lie, unfound wealth
can be focused—shared on display.

Grazing on Needles

My mother planted a pine tree for me when I was born. With outstretched hands tacked to its frame, a centurion rose from nothing. At this very time, little brown pine cone cows graze its verdant, lengthy tufts of green. The beasts pivot from the wind scudding by. Some even fall. A terse, humbled life comes to completion. Amber beasts sprawled out. A dry pan in afternoon sun. The local winds flow, cease. Fickle fingers loosen from their sockets. Hands—aloft—pour indigo rain onto our fallen. As each arrow leaves its lukewarm hive, the once-hallowed shapes wince. New born calves sit, waiting for next wind.

Keep Moving Forward

We're part of the extant few—you knew
this even before books began melting
into iPads, never leaving trails for anyone
to trace back. Forget the wasted efforts—
our map of the descent is too oblique.
Countless waves force and break
against themselves, never trying to return
crumbling relics to a half-decent state.
If we could go back to where the make
of things began, perhaps it wouldn't do us
any good at this point. Part of respecting
the past is letting it go.
When did we start this definitive regime
so consumed by its demand to live?
I celebrate its rest in my hand,
under my pen—full of sparks. I'll try
to make the best of it, one page
at a time, one section per day,
quick as hours, which in captivity,
live for years.

Ink in My Veins

In my own ink, what shall the soul
proclaim?
What's coded within the muse so hidden?
Secrets arise as energies untame
and relinquish notions of all that's
forbidden.
This blood of the page sings of the soul,
unleashing the tension of once closed
doors.
It allows a flow of spirit's voice whole—
cease-firing battles of internal wars.
With such serene words of caring digress,
perhaps noble regard and purest flame
will unite to produce seeds of finesse
whose same buds can find talents to claim.
Fuel forgotten fire concealed in niches.
Peace of mind brings forth untold riches.

Lacrimosa (for Upstate's Anatomical Gift Program Memorial Service)

They gave their vital tokens—all
bequeathed in spite of fear.
What once seemed a mortal fall
allows entry beneath veneer.

Keeping links between decades alive,
even if by some unique designs,
is essential for medical minds to thrive
and pick out those more delicate signs.

Subtle at first, these treasures give way
to seeing clearly what lies deep
inside our first patients on that last day,
honoring us with promises they'd keep.

No one here can say there will be
a time these memories won't aid
in lives we care for—burdens set free—
as we remark on sacrifices made.

Unlike many whose bodies have left
the watery eyes of those they love,
donors celebrated yet still bereft
will grace our minds while even above.

What Is Left Behind

There is still laughing
amidst the rooms we abandon.
There is still pounding
once our feet hold name-tags.
There is still insulting
perhaps even now,
with catacombs abound.
Maybe we can't stop
the endless memory
that spread itself
over the most delicate
artifacts of today.
Maybe this provides us
with the scaffold for change.

Unit 6A

Nurses on an ICU-overflow floor are stronger than people think. My experience—the first clinical mission of medical school—was built from their interactions. Following the so-called Queen of Comfort Care and her team of mixed professionals was humbling yet empowering. They carried the burdens of dealing with what the ICU didn't have time for by being benevolently sarcastic. It was like learning a new language. Even their phone calls were distinct.

"Can you pick up the line, Beth wants you?"

"Can you tell her I'm eating fruit?"

"Oh, I'll get right on that—pick up the damn phone."

Some doctors floated on by, not even piercing the surface of this humor. Some took part, talking about dogs and children. How else can you deal with the multitude of patients launched at you every few minutes? Making light of being a medical professional allowed them to reopen their minds.

"We have to schedule time to pee as nurses," the Queen lamented.

She dealt with a wavering patient lot that often changed moods more than their medications. Many did not appreciate the leering eye of medicine.

"Use the other guy, I ain't no guinea pig," one man told me.

Not all patients had this attitude. Plenty were just scared. One elderly woman, in a hospital for the first time, actually thought she was falling into her father's grave when being wheeled around in her bed. Surprisingly, younger patients were equally vulnerable.

"I just want to talk to someone who won't *judge* me because I'm addicted." said one woman.

This heroin addict—rather this woman addicted to heroin—was afraid and hurting more than I could know. She let me see how life had thrown her, left her alone, and offered few directions. Drugs helped her cope, but when the "good" drugs stopped, "bad" drugs filled their place—popping pills to snorting pills to injecting powders that would never be in pills. She may have been invaded, but she was not conquered, just trying to live again. I could see brightness in her eyes after someone listened and actually seemed to care.

I can't relate to her specific troubles, but I know what it feels like to fail oneself. Such an overflow of self-acrimony makes it seem impossible to find the right path. You can't even get a running start, let alone cross that bridge and reach the stream where your reflection is clearest. Medical school frequently makes me feel like I keep tripping as my speed increases, and the field I tread grows each month. How can I reach that precipice and leap to a place I've never been? It's a success story that I know will write itself, just like yours.

To Treat a Person Not an Addict

What if your name was told to you
before you entered waiting rooms?
What of gazes forlorn—thrown forth
that made our bodies feel like tombs?

Upon entry, all sigh to form ideas
whose bleeding hearts shine with hate.
A ripple of unease shrouds the abode
as if one's wounds could desecrate.

As fast as I could but reserved as well,
to her I routed my medical mind.
Ignoring the sunken holes in her arms,
I view—instead—shackles to unbind.

Let's try to make it better,
this talk and dance of claims.
I'll prod myself a little more
to pry apart these frames.

I might not know the trails
of rubble that tore your feet,
but I can adjust my sails
to find isles where we meet.

For each aching tear you shed,
I vow to keep stone-strong
enough to handle each strand of dread

revealing your life's song.

You have the strength inside
a place you have not known.
Unabated as it was before,
this area will soon be grown.

I cannot feel lost emotions
hidden in the years,
but I can attend to—lend myself
to your timorous tears.

Osmosis

Snow trickles down, slowly inching
so as to sneak past, forgetting
the cold country of their grandfathers.
Escape, melt away like liquid glass
as if it could send smoke signals
to that dubious dwelling. Maybe
pile together, pilfer some potential
from that watery composition—the one
you're always talking about.
You're past there, and this is now
equally untrustworthy.
Running up will only send you
back to where you first emerged.

Antonia

In the 1940's, the small town of Calabria, Italy housed a variety of locally owned farms and vineyards. The townspeople had no cars or any electronic appliances at all. Antonia's family was one of many who merely had a few lights that worked from six at night to six in the morning. Antonia never knew anything else but the simple, rustic lifestyle where bartering was predominant and money was sparse. She would walk for miles to reach her aunt's farm, surrounded by mountains and forest.

By the time Antonia turned sixteen, World War II had ended. The brown eyed girl yearned for a new life in an easier place. As she walked home after working on her aunt's farm, she often wondered what that great land would be like. One especially hot summer afternoon, she sat on a tree stump adjacent to her path home. She was about to chew an apple, picked earlier that day. After thoroughly polishing it, a glossy reflection stared back at her, revealing sweaty cheeks and messy, brown hair.

"Imagine what you could be, given the opportunity," she heard.

"I'd rather live," she thought aloud, "in a place where everyone has a chance to grow—to build a family. Somewhere with big houses, children all dressed up, where I can have a real pair of shoes."

That idea led her to a new life with plenty of surprises. Her children held her closely as she grew older and more extolled. Stories to her grandson became increasingly about that rustic home in Italy. To tell him about it was both nostalgic and heart-wrenching for her, but she found solace in the fact that he was her legacy.

That grandson would meet others from Calabria with a similar sense of humble optimism. The roughly translated maxim inscribed on its people read "hard-headed but strong of heart." If she could do it all over again, Antonia would still fall in love with the same German; she'd still choose the same life. Nevertheless, she dearly misses her home. It too has changed, and that almost hurts more than not being there.

Back to Basics

Do you know what makes us happy?
Are things so aptly named?
If one could blend the smallest parts,
they would surely not be tamed.

What if that's as simple as
the answer can really be.
Life is not components
but lithe with entirety.

We are what we think of
even if our falls are slight;
minor makings we call home
are in fact our light.

What, say you, is the cause
of pain and nouns we fear?
The simplest answer I can see
is not heeding whilst we're here.

We all want to be better
in more ways than one,
but it gets so much harder
under an unforgiving sun.

We must learn to forgive
without grudges or leers.
If not, each scar we own
will grow along our years.

Legless

The metallic prow of our vessel breaks the silence of the ocean as it emerges from the brooding fog. Crew members release sighs of relief as stale sweat evaporates off balding scalps. At last, the sun gives our bones some much needed warmth. I hold this new form of hope, waiting. Wanting more.

Still, I wish I could recollect how long we've been off land. I didn't dare ask anyone. Such queries would do us no good. At least not now. Instead, I fix my bronze eyes to the water, but uncertainty makes my hands uneasy.

I take a stab at mindfulness and become part of the present. Rote waves cheer as silver tips like razor blade edges slice through the air's lucid flesh. Each watery ripple seems conscious and directed. Pelagic pitchforks futilely pierce the sky as each crest raises. Fields of blue grass transform into tin soldiers each blindly following the sentinel preceding him.

One. Two. One. Two.

This peculiar tune grows ambient like a room filling up with smoke. I veer back to the hull and feel somewhat overwhelmed by the curt, violent splashes our blundering hulk of a boat makes. Men listen to the gulls beyond our sails, but all I hear are the waves screaming with antipathy.

I try imagining our ship, all bulky and gray, like some species of Viking leading his flock of brutes to battle. Vikings didn't ask, they ordered. That's what we were all right, a rioting vanguard crushing the aquatic foundation that was once unscathed. In place of innocence, we leave a trail of cork-colored waste and half-eaten dinners. Reluctantly, I watch my hands once more.

They suddenly feel bloody, maybe even perverse. There's a dance in my head each second, sorting through my vices and virtues like an elder Rabbi scanning the Torah for some answer he assumes has eluded him. Unlike most things, qualms can't be tossed over a boat. All I can do is keep trekking as far away as I can

Maybe the wind will grab my troubled notions like a bird caught in gale-force winds, imprisoned in constant duress.

Neptune's Loss to Athena

What can I say to the god of azure?
You drum up some water thinking it pure,
but the Athens-king did not find
that gift as worthy as another kind.
There are problems even gods can't cure.

Spring Rebellion Looks Decent
This Year

My sons of snow plant themselves
in chlorophyll igloos, releasing
their crimson. Ending so soon, turnover
spreads cold notions down
onto local cities that barely notice
the sunken wonders transforming
their acres of white into something
much more inviting.
In time, things would be
drastically different.

Daedalus' Envy

Her scarlet strands flow soft and flutter
over smoky mirrors on oceans blue.
They dance and dangle 'round beauty's
clutter
to flaunt the masterpiece that grants their
hue.
A slender statue draped in snowy gown
never needs motion to show her flight
as lingering zephyrs of her renown
hold fast my hoplites with brazened light.
Though time may lessen and ravage this art,
a part of her can never be faded.
She carries it with her—an abstract art
that lends itself to the fallen and jaded.
Though outer sheen shines brightest on
earth,
inside this creature is what holds her worth.

Freudian Slip

Consumed by some new brand of insecurity, a slightly-balding psychologist ruminated through his eyes, peeping at the ground for moments. These specs of solitude helped him hold his pieces together. Time had changed just then in the oncology lounge. This place appeared to be beyond his scope; attempts at consoling his completely valid concerns were futile. It didn't help that Wikipedia made small-cell lung cancer seem like the bubonic plague at best.

Waves of stinging obsessions spread like wild-fire until an unease permeated the room. His perfect troubles became opaque yet subtle enough to smell. Profuse drips of sweat just kept coming, disappointing considering how well he had been controlling his emotions. He even took a class for this kind of thing in grad school. He felt as naked to his bones as the exhibits that had once made him doubt creation.

Mental vespers went on repeat as he wished and prayed for some release—any relief. His breaths quickened. Then, someone in white placed their hand on his shoulder. The downward gaze told him that he had an ally. For once, safety felt assured.

He breathed and came back into what was now the present.

Slaughterhouse-Five

Only 5 pages in,
I'm surprised at Kurt Vonnegut.
What was expected, say the usual
character layout and arrangement,
was colorfully disarrayed into this
ardent mismatch of process
and present. Now and past were
so interwoven that I could not take
him without respect while still
admiring his unabashed playfulness.
I've heard of in media res, but Kurt—
well, he is a new breed. What is it
about Steinbeck's time that brought
so many minds into the clear fields
of glass that have today been turned
back into coarse sands and brush?

Widowed

I wrote a dazzling piece of soul.
It made me feel; it made me whole.
But the damned doc didn't save,
so in the streets of nothing I slave
to remember—renew—my withered goal.

Twenty-First Century

To us in this time-bond,
hurricanes must fall
into our circuits,
upgrade the so-called
imperious organ
systems we control,
and gently rock us
into numbing reveries.
We unpour our
post-spilling light
into heeding wind,
where our names
devotedly dissolve
pleading dreams
that minds ignore

My Scalp Is Red

I was a naïve, fragile child in fifth grade. My classmates were equally vulnerable. No one wanted to play basketball with the clumsy group they were assigned to, but our desires were ignored. The slovenly, broad-shouldered gym teacher bellowed words that struck us like hail. I wondered why he became a teacher. He wasn't; he was a real estate agent who got a gym teaching job at a private school. His mother was sick, and the school felt pity.

"We're breaking into teams for half-court basketball. I assigned your teams, so grab a jersey and start shooting. Come on, let's go!"

I nodded heavily, drawing my efforts to prepare for battle. The game started harmlessly, even though we were at the age where motor skills were just developing. It was embarrassing to be so ungainly. Lucky for us, we had no choice.

Passing went all right, but shooting was often accompanied by a mass of defenders falling into a misguided pile. We all went at the shooter simultaneously. He was the source of our potential defeat. Why not all attack at once?

40

After scores got close, the coach scoured for error. Considering our numerous mistakes, yelling increased. His raucous shouts made me yearn to crush the shooter at the next chance. The usual shooter—a larger-than-normal but not muscular kid—went up to shoot, and three children assailed his feet. The fray ended, yet I was in mid-run, mind stopping short while body kept going.

I collided head first with a door's corner. My writhing body was snatched up by the hand of the coach, indelicate as he was. My sobbing face went invisibly by, unnoticed by the motoring players. Keeping the tombstone of manhood nicely chiseled, his snarling disapproval was palpable. Whenever my eyes jumped to the face of the coach, his rigid features hardened into a derisive statue. It was a mistake to be a child.

I spewed unrecognizable sorrows, forced back against the walls of my stomach. When I grew especially perturbed, sizably noticeable, the sentinel would gaze over my chassis.

"You'll be fine. Stop crying," he commanded.

This was made prayer by my sympathetic overseer. His words burnt into vapor like dew in desert dawns. I kept on paining through the moment, waiting for answers. They came in rash, terse forms.

"My hand has blood on it when I touch my head…"

"Oh okay, fine. I guess you have to go to the nurse."

He had me stumble to the infirmary by myself. My vision was blurry, my gait like a drunk. I never made it upstairs. Bloody, red pools circled my mythical corpse. Of course I made it upstairs. I never had resolve like that before. Six stitches though.

Unwearied

Beneath carrions,
lies a plethora of green
waiting patiently.

Gut Feeling

With dalliance
    between my lungs,
this demure cadence
seems a subtle offing—
terse as passings that leap
to keep ships afloat.
A maelstrom of silent eyes
witness rain-drops
    hop on tree tops,
intrepid as breaths
composing their shapes.
We erase every notion
in the tempest, and yet
upon you, the elision
has moved only but an inch.

Grandma's Influence

Never once did I think
Nona's shadow would ever shrink
or weaken the hold it has on me
—in her eyes, God's face I see—
because with her, I'll always link.

Metanoia

Superlative injunctions sunk,
creeping into opulence. Then,
one note skipped—a new record
more burnished
than the last three.
Dawn smoothed up along
roaring barbs over
meager speech
drawn thin, within
deeper reaches.
The situation merely calls
for that brooding agility.
Will you hang
out vintage shingles or
use those craving alveoli?

Captive Audience

Looking, leap into yourself. Keep
the cold, yellow circle of empathy
alive, drawn inward
to quietly rebuild cities
as reflections echo like waves
between mountain tops.
Each ragged second splashes its way into
clouds.
The Atlantic came over the crop—that's all.
Now silver, a note plays;
        embers chatter
in the thicket where I lie,
inviting hoards of retinas
to whom I pour rosewood perils.

Catholic School Rumbles

My fight in second grade wasn't much of a fight. It was a falling of angels to earth. Charred wings were the source of sulfurous odor. The glittering eyes of bystanders could see a scene, if they chose to mark my existence. The only feeling—rather I should say sensation—was unpleasant. Then again, it was still recess after all.

Two boys sauntered over to where I half-stood, alone. I held up what I called a "helicopter seed." Two seed pods joined at a marginal border, allowing their fall from heaven to be that much more twisted. I would drop these crude twins into the caressing arms of wind—out of the superficial world I was confined to, at least for now.

My paired pods were dashed onto cold asphalt. The bodies of torn progeny lie peacefully to shrivel under an unforgiving sun. One boy, short with almost no neck to be found, whispered to his more bulky, masculine friend who spoke for the both of them.

"I want you to hit me."
"What?"

"You heard me. Hit me in the stomach with
fist."

"Will you leave me alone if I do?"

Instead of a response, the lackey of the duo helped me form a fist reluctantly. I pretended to move it forward, but before the action met completion, I was struck from behind by a clenched pair of hands. There's irony in a Catholic boy driving his hands prayer style into another boy's cervical spine.

I felt a mixture of anger, pity, and pain. They were just two carbon based amalgams bound together by mutual disdain, left to be fluttered helplessly in a wistful world. These two seemed like the samaras I had been so carelessly tossing.

At noon, I was called to the principal's office. I was seated, alone. The two boys had already said their side of the story, which must have included qualms in actually tattling on themselves. They said I started a fight. This daft notion struck me as inane, unbelievable to any administrator.

"So," the principal said after an interminable duration, "You hit a boy today. Is that right?"

My shock manifested as inorganic silence. This made me look guilty. I blurted out some spasm of words that seemed

49

appropriate given the curt thinking space I was provided.

"No, I just touched him—"

"Aha, so you did contact him!"

I yearned to curse the broken system, but it was not that simple. The first fracture was her loathing attitude toward someone who she had never met before. Her eyes beamed disappointment into the watery chasms of my soul.

"No! They came to me and said, 'Hit me.' I told them to please leave me alone, but—"

"Who in their right mind would ask such a thing?"

I was growing red, but I kept my feelings in as an energy that would diffuse through my life as works, as meetings, as kindness. Such a matrix might erupt from time to time, but I was learning to win the battles so common to the twenty-first century.

"They were bullying me! I just tapped his belly so he'd get what he wanted. I thought they would leave me alone if I listened to them."

"If this is true, why did you not get an adult?"

"I was scared, and the shorter one hit my back really hard. See?"

I attempted to reveal a mark where there was none. Semblances of fear floated in and boomed out. It made me lose faith.

"Get out. And don't let me find you back here or trouble will follow."

She wanted no part of truth, only order—as defined by a school.

The Time Traveler's Note

A letter stands there; its aim
I'm unsure of, but a tempting game
can't be resisted. Each line pours
my history through open doors,
swinging with efforts to reclaim.
There lies the spice of life inside
places we often choose to hide
from ourselves—and the world—
afraid of what might be unfurled
because we can't control the tide.

Dyspnea

She threw off the sheets, stomping on the floor in a frenzy. Each breath grew more intense and uncertain. Sensations of heat swept through, leaving behind a trail of freezing, acrid sweat. This was happening far too often and becoming far more uncontrollable. Should she call her daughters?

As she usually did, Barb grabbed the phone with one hand, held her chest with the other, and laid back down weeping as quietly as she could. Her husband, Robert, slept soundly beside her. She didn't want to seem weak. Or at least weaker.

She decided to call up her favorite coworker.

"Hi Margret...I know it's late but I had another
attack."

"Oh no, what happened?"

"I woke up with this searing pain and the feeling like my lungs weren't working. Like I had to push them open with force."

"Did you tell your husband?"

"He's asleep."

"You can't keep doing this to yourself. Needing

help doesn't make you any less strong."

Barb paused and held back a nervous tear. Guilt burrowed past the truth and stretched her emotional limits. Honestly, Barb wanted nothing more than to scream. She felt alone in the cold, unlit dawn. Her husband turned over.

Cognizance

The Eurasian prime minister gave up today.
It had taken years to get him
to merely allow water from outside the
motherland.
Prior to this time, immigrating water was
thought
to carry with it a plague of idiosyncrasies
                      —optimism, bias,
        faith—
that would indefinitely wash over the
pristine
homes of the townspeople and leave a
permanent coat
of foreign moisture. This pollution of mental
and physical
worlds was an affront to those in power.
Dilution of their principles was rapidly
preceded
by an influx of drought.

Senescence

You see
independence
can only stretch
so far
before doubling
back on itself
realizing the mortuary
is full of dreams.
I mean this
fortified headquarters
aligns just right. Naturally,
the universal problem
seems centered around
the decanted,
capacious reaping
of our unusable sustainability.

Skin

A crimson tear drop carries a dream,
a story, and a life. Every broken seam
springs into action each lilting brogue
of ancestors lost, both hero and rogue—
all of them wrapped in one giant ream.

Writer's Block

Writing just got hard. Not sure
when this started but the usual
twenty-four seems too little for me
to be able to conquer silence. Atrophy
becomes a novel yet fitting disguise
in the conquest for understanding.
Even hand-writing has gained
a cumbersome eloquence,
almost concealing my cause.
I mean that the act becomes
an interminable hike toward
drifting away from the prison
once urging my muse to sleep.
I wish I could say I'm not scared
because some deep valley echoes
my name in tones I never knew
could be uttered. If it was that easy,
words would lose color. Truly, each
of us can trace the ascent
written gently above. We
just have to stay aware.

Hephaestus

Who needs straight arrows?
I create automatons
crafting perfection.

Reflection

Inside a universe
of appearance,
beneath fuming silver,
looks out in anxiety
someone to vain
the shades of their soul,
listen to footsteps
echoing impatiently
within coils of madness,
and finally change
the purity of mirrors.

Diana

Is she really Apollo's sister—
the one unwavering eye?
Every arrow missed her;
the waterer did not lie.
Some plebian groups watch
myths come into being
yet carve within one notch
a doubt for all this seeing.
With tattered faces forward,
vociferous in our grasp,
unsure—we move toward,
until frozen inside collapse.
With heads spinning out,
our ears confuse the mind,
reminding us all about
the smallness of our kind.
Those deeds of both gods and men,
though questionable and seedy,
will turn the stones that line our pen
and make us feel less greedy.

Modern Extinction

Tiles at our feet dissolve
stone into clay.
A cooler of edged brews
or even a high-end future
cease together at the drip.
One delicate, naïve way
will—with each gulp,
each drowsy toll—
take its weight
and implant gravity
into the bones of children.
What was once a small crack
has turned out to be the end
for this poor, engorged egg.

A Shabby Ventricle

The imperial tyrant
that houses me plays
me like a spinet.
Amid every gauntlet,
in each realm afar,
climbing is burdened
upon myself.
For whom do my
interlaced fibers embraid
and twist in vain?
Am I a squire braced
against my own volition?
Why should this distorted state
be a terrace for beauty?
This business of being
a container for liquids
—variable concentrations—
rows and gleans
a spark of uncertainty
left behind in star-trails.
Though a dungeon,
this is still my home.

Fleeting

For those who say, "love is patient and
kind,"
I think they should keep three things in
mind:
love is wanting but cannot wait,
seizing the day, ignoring fate.
It will not yield to relentless terms
but must be molded as one affirms.
Guide love swiftly or be left to yearn
for what was truly yours to earn.

Returning

Upon second dash,
memory faltered
so as to allow my adoption
of life. There is tension building
when musicians brawl
toward the inevitable
compounds of society.
Continuing the rift coming up,
arises out of depths tumbling down,
the sanctifying reality wherein
writing stops being read
by hungry intellectuals.
It's a talk-and-dance; see
where some have landed
next to our own congruence.

Deforestation

Wakeful promises descend across valleys
torn apart like despoiled leather. Maybe
our semblances were not strong enough
to keep the ground in place. Maybe
our reckless vision kept the past
alive in the choices we made today.

A Fresh Start

This ink is new to me
as it flows out of the soul.
Not far, the two can see
how together they make whole.
This union of sense to logic comes
to birth inspiration's spark.
With such feelings, a new lyre strums
to awaken luminescence in the dark.

Unripened

I, warden, breathe
vicious lamentations over
freshly deloused numbers—
unionized like oranges,
languid
in their wicker basket.
Arrangement
carries little
to the picker,
placing them listlessly.
Scars circle
unadapted grasses.
Sallow steel eyes tumble
down glacial bricks,
controlled but helpless
in slothy gait.

The Man with Many Fedoras

When sullen smokes flitter wide,
dawn-speech coats the walls in pride.
Will you assemble lives of fright
to change each morning into night
or allow yourself to be our guide?

Cells

Hovering circles
pass through sliding veins nestled
in fancy design.

Sand Between Pages

There must have been
some granulated device
that snuck under and in
between flattening
and smoothening
stones of no luster,
only texture.
Life is uphill, past
the line of expectations,
beyond a starlit set
of tall, singing grass
where noise is dulled,
and scars can't last.
Lurid and somehow lost,
the hills rise and meet
other places not close
to this one beneath
our feet.

Hidden

She keeps so much tucked away,
it's hard to know what she'll display.
In either sense or any at all,
I know my words to her will crawl
and lay themselves as tokens of trust—
stepping stones to reactions robust.
Bedecked or gaudy works can't hold
a candlelight to what one can mold.

Someone Past

Like a dancer in the clouds,
she draws closer these crowds
of hemlock trees who wait
to be transformed and bait
true garden keepers, those
who saw that flowers rose
in the upmost canopy leaves,
where above, the sky relieves.
Let's just say those steamy eyes,
a worn-out past, can realize
that in dreadful deserts, water hides
beyond the purview of many guides.

Reputation

Sometimes, I grow
worried about how
to glorify the rocky
past I chiseled out
and placed in front
of us all to behold.
Immortality is funny
because it spans so
much more than fear.

After the Bombs Dropped

As desolate a place, it was safest here. We could move about within the confines of our town, but we had limits. Everyone knew each other. Everyone knew what not to say. And of course, everyone knew who was not allowed.

Hospitality was a luxury more than a responsibility. Over the past six months, we let in three new families and turned down upwards of sixty people. Solidarity was key.

At first, life was tolerable. Not great but sustained. Over time, diseases found their way in. They were always here, truly. We just never noticed. We started looking at books, but they didn't help all that much.

A physician made his way to our city. He was alone, covered head to toe in a variety of messy colors, some blood. I didn't want to know where the rest came from. He was quiet—not even that friendly, and yet I knew I'd never forget him.

"Hi there, could I make my way inside? My name is Marvin. I've been on the road for a while as you could probably guess. I'm not here to take anything, just to see if people need help."

"What kind of help are you offering?"

"I'm a doctor, and I'll bet you could use one of those."

"Am I supposed to believe you?"

"Do what you want. I just know this is what I'm good at, and if you don't want my help, I'll be on my way."

"Why bother helping people you barely know?"

"It's just what I was meant to do."

Made in the USA
Middletown, DE
16 October 2022